HOBSON'S CHOICE

BY NATHAN BROWN

GREYSTONE PRESS
EDMOND, OKLAHOMA
2002

Hobson's Choice
Copyright © 2002 by Nathan Brown
2nd printing 2003

All rights reserved
Printed in the United States of America

Library of Congress Cataloging-in-Publication Data
Nathan Brown, Hobson's Choice, poetry

Library of Congress Catalog Number
2002106370

ISBN: 0-9669-682-2-0
Softcover: alk. paper

Cover by Chris and Kelli Everett

Greystone Press
2220 N.E. 131 St.
Edmond, OK 73013
1-888-478-8189 or 405-478-8154 • Fax: 405-478-8153
Web: http://www.greystonepress.com

FOR SIERRA

TABLE OF CONTENTS

Acknowledgments ix
Preface xi
Introduction 1
Works Cited 21
Carp 25
3 Quarters 27
Beating the System 28
Black Stuff 29
Capitalism 30
Denied Space 31
Everyday Everytime 32
Homeless 33
Las Vegas 34
Whispers 35
Melting in the Pot 36
Or Current Resident 38
Purchase 39
She Tries 40
Suburba Pastora 41
The Maul 42
To - From 43
Traveler 44
TV 45
Two Tables Over 46
Chit 47
Baby Bumpy 49

Baudelaire's Angel	50
Flying	51
Her World	52
The Lucky Sock	53
Revived	54
Sweet Cakes	55
Din	57
Aliya	59
All Hayell!	60
Guns & Rabbis	61
Jericho	62
John the Southern Baptist	63
May Day	64
Southern-Fried-Sundays	65
Sunday Morning	66
The Wailing Wall	67
Moot	69
A Few Good Lines	71
Anything Goes	72
Award	73
Coffee	74
Compound Spiral	75
Emotion in Music	76
A Fitting End	77
Gematrias	78
Hobson's Choice	79
It's versus Its	80
Meaning	81

My Question to Freud 82

Openings 83

Orpheus Sing! 84

Point Blank Necrosis and Fugacious Concupiscence 85

Point Blank Murder and Temporary Sex 86

Rhetoric 87

Something 88

The Beast 89

The Villainous Nelle 90

Rumi 91

Ah, Thanksgiving 93

Ben Yehuda Street 94

Breath of Life 95

The Cool Winds Came 96

Cool, Cloudy 97

Depression 100

Evening / The Plains 101

Green Lady 102

Night Game 103

Perception 105

Sunset Symphony 106

Turkey Day 107

Wordless 108

Acknowledgments

To *Professor George Economou* — it was an honor to work with you. I feel very fortunate to have had a great teacher who is also a great poet. The guidance I received in your workshops and classes introduced me to new styles and writers that have continued to be primary influences. Also, I truly appreciate your understanding and patience during a rough time in my life.

Professor R. C. Davis-Undiano — many thanks for your tireless encouragement, straight talk, and for introducing me to the world of Chicano Studies. This body of literature has had a huge impact on my life and work.

Professor R. M. Davis — much appreciation for your honesty — sometimes brutal, but only when necessary — when it came to critiquing in the workshops. This combined with your sense of humor made the workshops a true joy.

Professor John Dunn — your kindness and laid back, unorthodox style guided me through my undergraduate work in linguistics. You made classes a pleasure and an adventure.

I would also like to thank *Professor David Gross* for the introduction to Walter Benjamin, sincere instruction, and the great talks about Bob Dylan, Bruce Cockburn and many others.

To *Clarissa Carr and Elyon Wall-Ellis* — for all the deadlines I would have missed . . . *thank you.*

Gladys Lewis, Laurie Polhemus & Molly Marzan at Greysone Press — for the bravery in publishing poetry. A possible qualification for sainthood.

Billy Crockett — for a powerful and poetic friendship like no other in my life.

Chris and Kelli Everett (and the Clovenator) — for your eyes and hearts. I look forward to our future. You are the original collage-jockeys.

Mom and Dad — Your patience, love, artistic natures, and tireless support are the reason I have had the freedom and privilege to pursue the path of education and creation. You have rescued me time and again. You have always been there. What else could I say?

Sierra — my daughter — I simply do not have words, Punkin. So, I offer the simple token of dedicating this book to you . . .

Preface

A book of poetry is not a travelogue. They have another section in the store for that. It is a crisis. Poetry is a precarious high-wire act of faith in words to reveal, to name, to remember, to whisper or shout the news of who we are, again and again. It is as necessary an item as is liable to be on any shelf in any store, with the possible exception of diapers and the blues. The foreknowledge of the dim state of poetry sales must be particularly liberating to the author. He may apply himself single-mindedly to the crisis at hand.

Nathan Brown's poems are experiments in soul-play. His keen eye for the hidden agendas of this world is tempered with a wink and the suspicion of joy. This collection of poems has suggested to me the idea of the poet-sleuth. See him there with one giant eye behind the thick rounded glass. He is always looking. Time may stretch out forever in the discovery of a certain "softness" or a slight catch in the breath. And that's not a problem because the poet's currency is time. It's not that he has any more of it than anybody else — he's simply chosen to spend it investigating the interiors and intimations of his world. He is always willing to see what he sees. Willing to give up the idea of "horseness" for the possibility of an actual horse, whatever that may be.

So who was Hobson anyway, and what was his dilemma? Turns out Hobson himself had no particular choice to make. An Englishman who leased horses to travelers, Hobson was famous for requiring his clients to take the horse nearest the door, whatever the condition. The phrase "Hobson's choice" has come to mean, therefore, a "seeming" choice where, in fact, there is no choice at all. I "chose" to drive the beat-up powder blue station wagon with the plywood back seat my granddad bought at a government auction. As a college student with little income, what were my options? One thinks also of the plight of the

American Indians "negotiating" for a life on the reservation. You take what you are handed.

So the irony is rich in the author's title. Bearing the inheritance of racial and economic privilege, he seems to enjoy a world of options. He may choose his career, his friends, his vacations, his schooling, his entertainment, his passion. He is only denied one thing — credibility. What a strange and silent barricade surrounds the poet from among the envied majority. He is given art schools and English degrees but no authorization to use his voice in the community. He has no right to speak according to prevailing sentiment. He has not earned it. He can take the lame horse closest to the door.

So what constitutes literary authority? All have experienced the glib misuse of language by those who don words like Easter bonnets — decoration for effect. Sarcasm and hard-selling pervade our culture from ad copy to the Sunday sermon. It is no surprise when language is employed to cover up motivations rather than reveal. Liza Doolittle responded best to this: "Words, words, words - nothing but words!"

What gives words significance? What gives them the capacity, the passenger space, to carry the reader to a place of meaning? It would seem to require a certain seed-like connection to experience. Life begets words. Some have posted their suffering on wailing walls and federal buildings with profound healing effect, to the shame of those who co-opt these words for commercial and political gain.

So who is entitled to write? Only those who live through great oppression and suffering? Only those who have been handed-off, ignored, mistreated and forgotten in the world? Certainly the community must hear from its unremembered self. But what about the voice of the middle class white heterosexual adult male who's never been to jail and does not find himself victimized, profiled or ushered into a symbolic role for the emergence of a minority power base?

There is no existential privilege for any of us. We are all given as a sentence and a birthright the task of making meaning of our short walk on this planet and our perfectly sure demise. In this we have equality. In this I am a brother to kings, serfs, and holocaust victims. All of our ears ring with the dizzy spells belonging to every human inhabitant of this spinning mother-ball in the Milky Way somewhere on its way to somewhere.

The authority to express derives from the human capacity to feel one's way along this world, to take notes, and to risk posting the results. And one more thing — one must love words when they do, sometimes, integrate and illuminate experience.

So maybe there is no choice for the poet after all. He sees something. He knows he must employ language. He must redeem words. And it is finally an issue of loyalty. He is credible, he is more than entitled, because he knows he is in the world for this — to name the animals, to respond, to evoke, to conflict, to defend, to risk, to honor. It is a high calling, not only to the oppressed, but to each of those rare and courageous beings of any age, color, creed and bank balance, willing to take up the life as well as the pen.

Billy Crockett

Introduction

Hopeful cynic.

    A colleague was brave enough to begin one of her works with a single self-descriptive noun. I had no choice but to add an adjective to mine. And as brief and simplistic as it may seem, I have needed quite some time to settle on this title. I did search—even hoped for—something more elevated, but none reflected as accurately my journey with literature and poetry.

I would like to be more impressionistic than I am with the images my words project or reflect. I often feel like an Abstract Expressionist when I am in the process of writing—loving nothing more than the sound, feel and appearance of letters and words on the page. But I usually pull out of this mode when I begin editing.

One movement that might begin to define my outlook is Minimalism. In my poems, I very much like to say as much as I possibly can in the fewest possible words. A comment I often receive about my songs is that they are too short. "You need another verse. You've got to add a bridge." I return, "But that's all I want to say." Anything more would amount to rambling.

A second possibility for expanding my self-definition is the Japanese aesthetic of wabi-sabi, a school of thought or aesthetic ideology, that has had a long association with the Japanese tea ceremony. Its three main tenets are:

> ...a beauty of things imperfect, impermanent,
>   and incomplete.
> ...a beauty of things modest and humble.
> ...a beauty of things unconventional (Koren 7).

Even the Japanese are at a loss for words to explain wabi-sabi, in part because those who most strongly adhere to its philosophical principles have deliberately avoided recording them in written form. Even a well-structured oral tradition of the approach is difficult to find. When those who *are* familiar with wabi-sabi speak about it, they avoid expressing themselves in rational or concrete terms. So, there's no way that I—a westerner born in the buckle of the Bible belt—could pretend to know or understand much about it. But there *is* an essence that Leonard Koren expresses in his book *Wabi-Sabi for Artists, Designers, Poets & Philosophers*, that helps me make sense of my ever-updating modes of thought. In wabi-sabi, there is an acceptance of degradation and contamination as natural processes within the course of life and beauty. The practice requires one to be intuitive and relative, as opposed to logical and absolute, and prefers rough edges and vague shapes to perfect lines and precise representations. My mother, an impressionistic artist, describes the essence in her work as "lost and found edges." For me, wabi-sabi helped clarify my already existing feelings that *good* and *bad* are not divided by a line drawn between people groups. Instead, they exist in and around a blurred line that runs down the middle of every human being. This is the way I see life and art. Beauty and love are everywhere—even among all the ugliness and hate.

When I was eight years old, John Denver's crackly *Rocky Mountain High* LP infected me with a disease from which I never recovered—a desire to play guitar and sing for people. No matter how many years have passed since I last sang the song, I can always drum up the words, "He was born in the summer of his twenty-seventh year..." without having to think about it at all. I ached to be able to play and perform songs like "Annie's Song" and "I'm Sorry." I could say it was the simple poetry in the lyric. I could say it was the fact that the guitar chords are playable where a novice is concerned. I could also say it was because I wanted girls hanging all over me. But it doesn't matter, I suppose, when it all eventually leads to a life of never being able to read or write enough literature and poetry.

John Denver is so important in my situation because he granted a first step—one which led to Gordon Lightfoot and James Taylor—who in turn led to Bob Dylan, Paul Simon, Bruce Cockburn and Sting. These songwriters inspired me to become a songwriter myself. I loved their music. And because of that, I began to listen closely to their words.

So, outside of a few of Edgar Rice Burrough's Tarzan novels during kid-hood, a sinfully enjoyable romp with J. D. Salinger's *Catcher in the Rye*, brought on by a gorgeous tenth grade teacher, I really can't say too much about the impact of books on my earlier life. I know I loved books. I know my parents read to me. But I can't drum up specific titles. Music single-handedly jump-started my initial interest in the arts.

I attribute almost solely to Sting my decision to return to college and study linguistics and English. His lyrics stood out to me as being more unique and much deeper than most other artists I enjoyed. He made me work to understand his lyrics. He forced me to look up words in the dictionary and mythological gods in the encyclopedia, heaven forbid. I wanted to know what he was up to with lyrics like:

> The boy child is locked in the fisherman's yard
> There's a bloodless moon where the oceans die
> A shoal of nightstars hang fire in the nets
> And the chaos of cages where the crayfish lie
>
> Where is the fisherman, where is his goat?
> Where is the keeper in his carrion coat?
> Eclipse on the moon when the dark bird flies
> Where is the child with his father's eyes?
>
> (Sting, "The Soul Cages")

So, I did some biographical research and discovered he had an educational background in literature and poetry. I then found out he'd also been a schoolteacher in Newcastle, England, for several years before joining The Police. Through this research, I realized I wanted to learn to write words that painted dark and beautiful pictures, as Sting does in "Fragile,"

> If blood will flow when flesh and steel are one
> Drying in the colour of the evening sun
> Tomorrow's rain will wash the stains away
> But something in our minds will always stay
>
> (Sting, "Fragile")

I knew I had to get back to school and study the masters.

Through studying these and other such lyrics, I began to contemplate the mysterious power of metaphor on a deeper level. I wanted to learn about its ability to communicate so much more than the journalistic quality of the *straight story*. Metaphor seemed to drop the presumption that a writer could give plain answers to what we all find out in the end are circular, unanswerable questions. Sting proposed the idea that it's better to speak artfully *of* a person or story than to speak *at* or definitively *about* them. Lyric and poetry function on a higher level when they *suggest* as opposed to *define*. This might be painfully obvious to some. But it was a bright and shining revelation for me at the time. Sting's influence has stayed with me, and I appreciate his never-ending commitment to fly in the face of what is *in* and *selling* in the suffocatingly commodified pop music scene. And as I grow older, I sense a softness and meaning in his words that only grow in their ability to speak to me…

> He deals the cards as a meditation
> And those he plays never suspect
> He doesn't play for the money he wins
> He doesn't play for respect
> He deals the cards to find the answer
> The sacred geometry of chance
> The hidden law of a probable outcome
> The numbers lead a dance
>
> (Sting, "Shape of My Heart")

When Sting forced me back into college, I had a second awakening in my journey with the arts. Linguistics built my foundation. The problem was that when I finally got to the English department for my master's, I quickly realized I was coming in with a severe handicap—I simply was not well read enough in the English canon to carry on an academic conversation. The size of many of these books, combined with the fact that I'm a slow, laborious reader, terrified me.

Through facing this fear, I began the slow, life-defining process of discovering my own voice. I started with listening to the voices of others from a classical past.

One of the earliest voices I encountered was Dante Alighieri. Although his trilogy *The Divine Comedy* is his most recognizable work, it was his first work, *Vita Nuova*, in which I felt so at home with his desperation and awkwardness in matters of youthful love and the general debacle of social interaction:

> Since this was the first time her words
> had ever been directed to me, I became
> so ecstatic that, like a drunken man, I
> turned away from everyone and I
> sought the loneliness of my room,
> where I began thinking of this most
> gracious lady and, thinking of her, I fell
> into a sweet sleep, and a marvelous
> vision appeared to me. (5)

This suffocating difficulty in communicating with fellow human beings, particularly those of the female persuasion, at an early age was a powerful touchstone between Dante and me. His adolescent tendency to magnify what to most people would be everyday encounters and circumstances to epic proportions gave me tremendous reassurance. As a matter of fact, the similarities in our youths struck such a chord, I almost felt ordained to writing.

Along with being an introduction to early epic poetry, *The Divine Comedy* also gave me a lasting allegory for the arduous patience and eternal effort required of the poet. The work illustrated the idea that a certain degree of ignorance about the future, combined with a firm hope for, and faith in, final outcomes, is at times all that keeps us going. The poetry also served to reinforce my suspicion—initiated by Sting—that the heart of deeper communication lies in mastering the use of metaphor. Beautiful and thought provoking metaphors seep out of Dante's lines.

Certain lines taught me about artistic freedom. Take the single phrase from *The Inferno* that refers to Barbariccia's fart blast from the "trumpet of his ass." (Canto XXI, Line 139) How liberating this line was at the time I encountered it! It helped me uncork my own a bit and led me to contemplate the idea that the artist should always work with a bit of a smile at the corner of his or her lips. Taking oneself too seriously is a common crime in the profession of the arts.

On a larger scale, *The Divine Comedy* served to launch a very personal investigation into the belief system of my youth and young adulthood. It didn't bring about a complete denouncement of my Baptist heritage, but I did begin a process of intense reassessment. It had a lot to do with the astounding degree of "para-scriptural" liberty Dante took in relaying such an expansive vision of Hell, Purgatory, and Heaven. I was forced to rethink my stance on the nature of revelation. I realized I'd been operating on an assumption that God's interaction with humanity, in the form of divine inspiration, had somehow ended with the final book of the New Testament. And, for the life of me, I could no longer *imagine* why this would be the case. If *The Divine Comedy* was not "divinely" inspired, then where did it come from? Was it a delusional dream of amazingly poetic and epic proportions? On the other hand, if it was divinely inspired, what reason could we possibly give for not including such a profound vision in the Bible itself. This crisis, brought on by Dante, turned out to be a critical turning point in my life, as well as my writing.

John Milton's work lit the fire of argumentation and editorial in me. His essay, "Areopagetica," proved to me that strong stances on ageless issues can be as useful hundreds of years later as they are in the time they are written.

Most notable though, was the fuel that Milton's work, namely *Paradise Lost*, added to the spiritual fire sparked by Dante. Even though I didn't agree with him on many counts, he kept me pinned to the wall when it came to continuing to reassess certain aspects of my beliefs and the nature of revelation. As devout as I was in my religious convictions at the time, I was again amazed at the extensive poetic liberties taken in describing an epoch that is only vaguely referred to in the scriptures.

Outside of encounters in poetry, none was as powerful as Walter Benjamin. His fascination with fragments, or what those writing about him later came to call "thought images," helped me see that there was precedent for the way my mind works when it comes to taking in, processing, and then expressing information and ideas.

The sheer volume of what is available in literature is so overwhelming it sometimes discourages me from even starting that next book or reading project. And for all the preliminary weeding that has to be done, simply deciding *which* book should be next can waste precious time. Benjamin's writings showed me I was not alone in my frustration and offered some much-appreciated affirmation and meaningful tools to help me deal with these problems. The affirmations were numerous, but are summed up in this quote from his essay "N [Re the Theory of Knowledge, Theory of Progress]" in the *Arcades Project*:

> Since the rise of the mass press, an overview of the sources has become impossible. [N 4a, 6] (Smith, 54)

He helped me see that collecting the outstanding nuggets—beautiful bits and pieces—found in literature and poetry was not only acceptable, but in some cases may actually be the only way to experience the essence of some works and time periods. I'll never give up on my life-long effort to read as much as I can, but with the prolific activity of mass production, there is no conceivable way one human being could cover it all. In his "*Introduction to* Central Park," Lloyd Spencer wrote, "In a century replete with esthetes of the fragment, Benjamin was its most demanding, stringent, expressive connoisseur"

(31). In Benjamin's essay "N," he describes fragments in more poetic terms:

> In the fields with which we are concerned, knowledge (*Erkenntnis*) exists only in lightning flashes. The text is the thunder rolling long afterward. [N 1, 1] (43)

Benjamin's need to listen acutely for every "accidental quotation" and "fleeting mention of a book" over the course of his lifetime is a feeling I've experienced, as well as acted on, for quite some time now. And the *Arcades Project* provides a model for the manner in which I have been going about it. This multitudinous collection of excerpts and quotations reveals his all-consuming penchant for the "lightning flashes" of knowledge and wisdom. It was his firm belief that in the age of mass press, gleaning the fragments may become an absolute necessity—possibly the only way in which we will be able to deal with truth, philosophy, and history.

Fragments operate on another level for Benjamin, a deeper one that has been very influential in the process of selecting material for my poems. This is the realm of brief moments and events in life that give expression to the inexpressible. Benjamin seems very concerned with this aspect of existence in his essay, "The Storyteller: Reflections on the Works of Nikolai Leskov:"

> The insight which grasps this unity … becomes the divinatory-intuitive grasping of the unattained and therefore inexpressible meaning of life (99).

If we pay close attention to life, it may repay us with fleeting glimpses of truth and hope that will unfold before our eyes in day-to-day situations. One of my favorite descriptions of this is in the essay "Theses on the Philosophy of History" in *Illuminations*:

> a conception of the present as the 'time
> of the now' which is shot through with
> chips of Messianic time (263).

These "chips" are the moments, events, and words that enable us to perceive, as Dr. David Gross put it, "the untouchable truth brushing by us, breathing on the back of our necks."

In fiction writing, I can see where the influence of a few specific writers might be the driving force behind a new writer's development of style and voice. But poetry is not as simple to define within these lines. So many individual poems from so many different writers have influenced me. I might begin with Paul Blackburn who introduced me to the strength of the short phrase in poetry. I saw how a few well-constructed words could communicate as well as, if not better than, a lengthy phrase. Among my favorite examples are his poems "Paris, and Not Spring Either," "Good Morning, Love!" and these wonderful words from "La Lisière" in *The Selected Poems of Paul Blackburn*:

> How we move
> about the wealth
> of friendships :
> too often at the edge of it
>
> How rare, the move to center
>   Where we live (250)

In the poem "Remains of an Afternoon," he shows that brevity, where the entire poem is concerned, can communicate volumes. These discoveries were very important to me during the early stages of my writing and reemphasized the thoughts Walter Benjamin had recently sparked in my mind.

I also appreciated the realization of the freedom the poet ultimately has when it comes to manipulating or breaking with form.

Little doubt exists about Blackburn's understanding of the forms and "rules" of poetry. Yet, he had no problem breaking them when he wanted to make a point or share a new vision for the ways in which words could be put together and placed on the page. Blackburn's poem "Structural" inspired "Baby Cakes" in the "Chit" section of this collection. After spending some time with his poem, I realized he meant for it to be read from the bottom up. This inspired me to try and write a poem that could be read in both directions—top to bottom, and bottom to top. I attempted this by describing my daughter and her crib in terms of layers, like a multi-tiered cake. Although the core of what I wanted to say in the poem works best when read from the bottom up, it still seems to work from top to bottom.

From Blackburn's work, I also explored the way unused space on the page is able to communicate. The spaces and indentations in the poem "Phone Call to Rutherford" actually cause the words and syllables to stutter in this record of a brief phone conversation with recent stroke victim, William Carlos Williams:

"I have dif-fi /   culty

        speak-ing, I

cannot count on it, I

am afraid it would be too em-

       ba

        rass-ing

for me ." (111)

I feel the struggle and sense the stammering without having to hear the poem read aloud. The white spaces and line breaks speak of the tortuous trip-ups and pauses in the speaker's brain. Accomplishing this without actually telling the reader this was a stroke victim was terribly impressive to me.

I also appreciated the confirmation that spelling is relative when sound is more important. The mannerisms and moods conveyed in the sound of a person's voice could greatly diminish the number of written words necessary to understanding a piece. A favorite example where this is concerned is "It Might as Well Be Spring":

> "Ven I kom to dis country
> skirts vair *dis* high
>
>   (the hand)
>
> und vit a slit, yet, in da zide,
> up to *here!*" (114)

The nationality and conservative nature of the speaker doesn't need to be explained. The *sound* of the language is adequate. This reiterated the thought I encountered with Sting, that one of poetry's true calls is to "suggest" or make evident *without* explanation and definition. Blackburn used this tool to the extent that, at times, I had difficulty understanding some of his poems at all. But how can I fault a guy who had the foresight to include in one of his pieces this nugget, referring to one of my professors:

> My friend, Economou, a medievalist
> and poet, owns the most spec-
> tacular Afro I've ever seen . (229)

I would be remiss if I did not discuss the contribution Latino, and more specifically Chicano, poets have made to my love for poetry. I've always had a secret romance with all things Hispanic. I've also had a strong desire to learn the language—though I struggle with it for lack of opportunity to practice. Since I have no genealogical excuse and very little experiential justification, I can't explain this mysterious affinity. But it exists, quite genuinely, nonetheless. I didn't voice my love for these poets in the early years for fear of it appearing manufactured. However, the relationship has carried on long enough now that I feel comfortable coming forward.

Early on in writing workshops, I was introduced to Frederico García Lorca and Octavio Paz. These encounters led to a personal investigation into other poets such as Pablo Neruda and Anthony Machado. Later, through a series of courses on Chicano studies, I came across Sandra Cisneros, Ana Castillo, Pat Mora, and have since had the privilege of meeting Denise Chávez, Demetria Martínez, and Rudolfo Anaya.

The subconscious pull into this realm had a lot to do with the energy and urgency that inevitably bubbles to the surface in a culture faced with extinction. A profound honesty often comes over a people faced with drastic, tradition-threatening change. An honesty and urgency pour out of a writing culture that *truly* has something at stake. And it is this very quality I find excruciatingly absent in so many contemporary poets in the mainstream-white-male culture that I'm unavoidably strapped to. Thus, the title of this collection, "Hobson's Choice."

There may be a shaky simplicity at times, even a lack of technical or academic ability, in some Chicano literature. I'm not remotely qualified to make this kind of judgment. At the same time, if Sandra Cisneros, Demetria Martínez and Denise Chávez are not poets of the highest order, someone would have to explain it in terms I could understand. Every time I entertain the briefest thought that I'm becoming a decent poet, I reread Demetria Martínez' "Breathing Between the Lines," or Sandra Cisneros' "Woman Hollering Creek," and promptly step back down from the pedestal. Both poets carve out and serve up metaphors so rich, I can't decide whether they inspire or frustrate me. Of course, it's both. One example might be this stanza from Martínez in the poem "Rally":

> now clouds with their manes and black nostrils
> tuned to the whip of your voice race south
> hauling faxes, press releases (41)

Put simply—and with a healthy dose of hopeful cynicism—what they are doing *matters* to them. I want that. I'm sick to death of the postmodern (whatever that turns out to mean) fallout that engulfs my generation. It's a seemingly terminal condition in which nothing can be allowed to be "all that interesting." Nothing can matter too much. And, even if it does, it can't be allowed to matter past a certain amount of stingily allocated time. Noteworthy works seem to take on some kind of brow-crinkling, antediluvian quality within a couple of months or even weeks after their release. This condition may be more prevalent in the music world. But I believe it's very much at work in all the arts today.

I want my poetry to *matter*, at least to me. I want to be a part of activating change within a culture that is decaying into a terrifying apathy. I may be miles away from being this kind of poet, but it's where I want to go. In "The Storyteller," Walter Benjamin claims that it is the "nature of every real story [to contain] something useful" (86). I owe a considerable debt to the Latino and Chicano writers for bringing me to my place of passion, my dream for usefulness.

In the eleventh hour of my formation, Charles Baudelaire strolls across the stage—leaving me curious as to where he's been all my life. When I picked up "Les Fleurs du Mal," the first two lines of the first poem, "Consecration," told me I'd have to read on:

> When by an edict of the sovereign powers
> The Poet enters this indifferent world, (11)

Stanzas six and seven in this same poem inspired the latest addition to my collection, "Baudelaire's Angel," to the extent that I had to include an epigraph.

If I had come across Baudelaire too early in life, I may not have been able to take the suffocating depression and stygian licentiousness that pervades the poems he calls "sickly flowers." But with an honest assessment of the plague of institutionalized religion in my life and culture, the general realities of growing older, and a quasi-successful graduation from my divorce, I've come to love the messiness of life and, what I often refer to as, the wabi-sabiness of it all. Beauty simply *is not* possible without imperfection. And without the mirror of depravation and evil, there would be no way to see the reflection of truth and love.

Baudelaire passionately paints the underlying beauty of beggars and street dwellers in poems like, "To a Red-Haired Beggar Girl" and "The Seven Old Men." In the poem "The Little Old Women," he describes the "charming refuse of humanity" in terms of a sad, involuntary dance. His passion was such that he would follow these people around in the streets, observing them at great lengths. Although I wrote it before my encounter with Baudelaire, my poem "Homeless" reveals the early stages of very similar feelings on my part.

In hearing his words:

> To heaven where he sees a splendid throne
> the oblivious Poet lifts his pious arms,
> and blinding flashes of his intellect
> keep him from noticing the angry mob: (12)

I not only find a beautiful statement on the nature of the poetic process, but also see the influence of Baudelaire on Walter Benjamin with his "lightning flashes." Benjamin leaves little suspicion as to the impact Baudelaire had on him in essays like "On Some Motifs in Baudelaire," from the book *Illuminations*.

The last two stanzas in "Epigraph for a Banned Book," the closing poem of "Les Fleurs du Mal," give me great solace when it comes to the plight of being misunderstood, and all the other insecurities attached to writing poetry:

> If, however, your impassive eye
> can plunge into the chasms on each page,
> read on, my friend: you'll learn to love me yet.
>
> Inquiring spirit, fellow-sufferer
> in search, even here, of your own Paradise,
> pity me . . . If not, to Hell with you! (176)

Albeit "in the face," these words speak to the egomaniacal inner voice that some artists must listen to in order to have the courage to wake up the next day—let alone create again.

Baudelaire speaks to the beginning of the rest of my journey with poetry. It's time to *get reading* and find as many more "fellow-sufferers" as possible—laughing and weeping with them all along the way.

So many artists have been influenced by relationships with other contemporaneous artists. These relationships exist in various forms, from that of equitable buddies hanging out in mutual friendship, to student/mentor situations, as well as everything in between. The dervish mystic and poet, Rumi, had Shams of Tabriz. Monet had Pisarro. Hemingway had Fitzgerald—or maybe it was the other way around. But these pairings are undeniable when it comes to the weight of their impact on the works of those involved.

In light of this, I would like to mention one such relationship.

Some artists are lucky enough to meet and become friends with one of those they most respect in their field. When it comes to songwriting, I've been one such lucky person. Billy Crockett is well known in many musical circles as one of the finest acoustic guitar players in the business. And for those who have grown weary of wading through monolithic piles of nonsense, when it comes to lyrics in today's music, Billy's words offer a philosophical and social landscape that is flooded with intent, desire, and intense commitment to craftsmanship. I've always kept an eye and ear on his work when crafting my own. His words, and at times frustrating ability on guitar, have served as a watermark for my writing.

Although lyric—unaccompanied by its music—usually looks like a model posing uncomfortably in the nude, I believe it is important to include a few snapshots of Billy's work that illustrate what I've shot for over the years:

>   For every life dry as dust
>   Blown to the edges where dreams are lost
>   "Mercy as the Rain" from *Watermarks*

>   This is the drum on a distant rise
>   This is the smoke of a sacrifice
>   This is the howl in a voice that cries
>   You can't harbor love
>   This is the flash in the thunderhead
>   This is the rush in the watershed
>   This is the hymn playing in my head
>   It's all or nothing
>   "Love the World" from *Simple Plans*

As I now turn toward writing in a more general sense, I am grateful for the way in which my friendship with Billy has begun to expand and deepen. Although songwriting is still very important to me, the emphasis has shifted from musical performance to all things written. I still consider Billy somewhat of a mentor. But our discussions and times together have now taken on a new, more vibrant quality that revolves around much more than music.

The infinite universe of poetry is new to me. It stretches out before me as a massive project that ensures I'll have something to do for all the remaining hours and minutes of my life. And while all of these influences—many of which remain unmentioned for lack of space—are, and have been, crucially formative elements, I still believe my journey has consisted more of a sense of identification with the spirits of great writers than a painstaking deconstruction and analysis of their style or technique with the intent to mimic. I simply cannot get enough. I learn by osmosis. This may be good or bad. I don't know. But this is the way I see it ... and write it.

Nathan Brown

WORKS CITED

Alighieri, Dante. *The Divine Comedy: Inferno*. Trans. Allen Mandelbaum. New York: Bantam Books, 1982.

—. *Vita Nuova*. Trans. Mark Musa. Bloomington: Indiana U P, 1973.

Baudelaire, Charles. *Les Fleurs du Mal*. Trans. Richard Howard. Boston: David R. Godine, 1997.

Benjamin, Walter. *Illuminations.* Trans. Harry Zohn. Ed. Hannah Arendt. New York: Schocken Books, 1969.

Blackburn, Paul. *The Selected Poems of Paul Blackburn.* Ed. Edith Jarolim. New York: Persea Books, 1989.

Crockett, Billy, and Milton Brasher-Cunningham. "It All Turns." *Simple Plans.* Walking Angel, 1999.

—. "Love the World." *Simple Plans*. Walking Angel, 1999.

—. "Mercy as the Rain." *Watermarks*. Walking Angel, 1998.

Denver, John, and Mike Taylor. "Rocky Mountain High." *Rocky Mountain High*. RCA, 1972.

Koren, Leonard. *Wabi-Sabi for Artists, Designers, Poets & Philosophers*. Berkeley: Stone Bridge P, 1994.

Martínez, Demetria. *Breathing between the Lines*. Tucson: U of Arizona P, 1997.

Smith, Gary, ed. *Benjamin: Philosophy, Aesthetics, History*. Chicago and London: U of Chicago P, 1983, 1989.

Sting. "Fragile." *...Nothing Like the Sun*. A&M, 1987.

—. "Shape of My Heart." *Ten Summoner's Tales.* A&M, 1993.

—. "The Soul Cages." *The Soul Cages*. A&M, 1991.

carp

3 Quarters

she didn't look to have a dime
to her brown   scarf   name

but she must have had
at least a couple
of crumpled up dollars
left over
from the welfare check

she bought the breakfast special—
scrambled eggs n' pancakes

after tax
she got 3 quarters back

with those she played
the jukebox—

Rosemary Clooney
       got the feet tappin'

The Beatles
       cracked a smile

n' Ol' Blue Eyes
       made us both cry

Beating the System

The air warmed back up today—
good for workin' in the attic.

Went to Radio Shack.
Bought a cheap antenna.

Gotta false sense
of beatin' the system—
sort of a legal,
wimpy Robin Hood.

"Damn the cable!
Won't pay it!"

Anarchists start
with baby steps too.

Black Stuff

they look
happy.
he's older, grayer
in a black shirt n' jeans.
she's younger, blonder
in a black shirt n' jeans.

he talks on a black cell phone
pulled from a black briefcase.

she writes in a notebook
pulled from a black bag.

he's on hold.
so he talks about bills n'
credit cards n'
operating in the black.

he talks about interest
on her account.

they kiss
n' talk about a white wedding.

they look
in separate directions
n' wonder
who'll get all the black stuff
if it doesn't work out.

Capitalism

So—
I'm ridin' public transportation,
a half-hearted finger at the bourgeois,
but

thinkin'
"I'm a new home-owner."
       as if anyone can own
       anything,
knowin' even my three jobs
won't pay for it.

I'm seein' Stafford Loans
in the grinding teeth
of 5th and 6th year seniors.

I'm smellin' stale turkey
from a leftover Subway shirt.

I'm listenin' to the bus driver
talk about how he's afraid—
afraid of losin' this job,
       as if he'd lost several.

I'm lookin' at his white hair…

Denied Space

A dry wind blows

on civilization

```
  ‾ ‾
|  NO   |
| PARKING |
  _ _
```

signs

jerk in the gusts

a rattling anthem

Everyday   Everytime

art dies   everyday   everytime

    Mozart   repeats on the radio

art dies   everyday   everytime

    Monet   becomes a postcard

art dies   everyday   everytime

    Rodin   is reduced to plastic

art dies   everyday   everytime

    Shakespeare   is slapped on celluloid

art dies ...

Homeless

They sit by the night-time blue
of Honolulu's sea
a bench   on the boardwalk
of pacific Waikiki
laughingly inhaling
familiar brackish air   strangely
sardonically happy.

    Across the street
    through the windows
    of a second story ballroom
    the dull yellow of crystal chandeliers
    barely reveals the red and white helium
    bubbles   tied to the backs of chairs.

Maybe the couple is secretly laughing
at those poor bastards up there
in their cumbersome clothes
of black and white pomp
and dreadful ceremony
dancing to a third rate cover band
that can't drum up their favorite tune.

Las Vegas

Pair o' dice
 Lost

Whispers

Father Culture
whispers in my ear,
spitting out seeds onto concrete,
"Take it—
the planet was made
for you."

Mother Earth
whispers an older story
that reeks of lost truth,
seeps in through pores—
an ancient reminder—
       "only so much …"

Melting in the Pot

So—

I'm riding home from class,
the usual random route.
Today it leads me by
the Midway Market & Grocery,
Eufala Street and Chautauqua.

I pass a chinless man
who chomps a recent purchase
like hay in a hippo's mouth.
His wrinkles, eyes n' glasses
suggest a chest of tales.

Further down the road
I spy a young driver
wielding a Nippon box
with Tinker Toy wheels,
rebel flag in front,
Scottish seal in back.

I run the pinkish light,
cross a busy lane.
A big white Dodge passes—
a pickup made for cowboys—
but driven by a turban
and a raging Muslim beard.

I turn down Iowa Street,
cross some hidden border—

a rio not so grande
anymore—
and smell the cooking
corn tortillas—
fruit of sacred, devouring dirt—
that bless Chicano stoves.

But—
what truly turns my head?
A frayed and tattered flag,
the stars and stripes of home,
blowing starchy in the breeze,
        up-side-down.

☒☒☒☒☒☒-☒☒☒☒☒@☒☒.☒☒☒

(or current resident)

---

a thin slice of blue pie
in a phosphorescent screen
becomes an attachment
reflecting red bottles

it spills into raging fiber
flashes into the depths
for three nano-days
and two nano-nights

only to rise again
in another gleaming screen
reflecting
that same Tabasco tie

Purchase

i pop into Target
on a pain fully muggy afternoon—
one of those must-do purchases
i never want to take time for.

i'm lost as i roam the renovated aisles.
nothing is where it had been
    when i bought my orange skate-board
        23 years ago.

at the bright red counter
i thought fully spill blue n' yellow items
    —a spray-can of WD-40
        Household n' Automotive Lubricant
    —Preparation H® Hemorrhoidal Suppositories.

avoiding the pitying posture and gaze
of the sigmoidally sound sales clerk,
the epiphanal thought suffuses my mind—

    "One way 'r another, baby…

        one way or another."

She Tries

she tries so hard to fill

s p a c e s   left

by a
        psychotically religious   mother
and a
        religiously psychotic   father

she   tries so *H*arrrrd

    to smoo**t**h   out th*E* rough p*L*aces

                      in her *P*<u>l</u>ast

allforthehopeofalittlecontinuity

something
        someone
                she can count on

but
        walls…
                the walls…

Suburba Pastora

You're next!
Oh verdant field of my childhood.
You are next,

Oh remnant of the once Great Plains,
Home of the fiery cardinal.

My tears wet your sandy belly,
Pregnant with concrete and brick.

You are next,
Oh friend of better days.
You're next.

The Maul

the hook sets
deep in the throat
of the need to possess

silver n' gold
lusty shine
deadly grip
hand   stuck in the jar

sticky walls
plastic motel
a flutter of limbs
the final throes

people of fashion,
taste and intelligence
haul it all back to the cell
hang it   store it
            ∾ the fish flips back in the sea ∾
hide it   hoard it
            ∾ the monkey n' cockroach run free ∾

To – From

noisetalkingnewsblaringhornshonkingdogsbarkingkidsscreamingbabiescryingdrillsdrillingjetsroaringdriversyellingsirenswailingradiosblastingspeakersthumpingtirescreeching alarmsringingengines r u m b l i n g f a n s h u m m i n g
w a t e r d r i p p i n g c l o c k s t i c k i n g
c r i c k e t s c h i r p i n g
b r e e z e s w h i s p e r i n g

wilderness

silence

revelation

wisdom

w h i s p e r i n g
b r e e z e s c h i r p i n g
c r i c k e t s t i c k i n g c l o c k s dripping waterhummingfansrumblingenginesringingalarmsscreechingtiresthumpingspeakersblastingradioswailingsirensyellingdriversroaringjetsdrillingdrillscryingbabiesscreamingkidsbarkingdogshonkinghornsblaringnewstalkingnoise

Traveler

A jacket
On a broomstick
Slumped in another
Useless heap
In a foreign
Border town

He only wants
To get back home
But he's currently
Misunderstood
In three different
Languages

The villagers
Would pay his way
Just to get rid of him
But they don't have
The money either

Maybe they
Were on their way
Somewhere
One time
Too

TV

Another Saturday Night
Live,
Chris Farley hosting.

I sit,
as the week unbuttons its shirt,
proving the average American
is a blue-light special
Wal-Mart bowl
of slowly cooling
Hamburger Helper.

Two Tables Over

a guy with black hair
black T-shirt
black tennis shoes
a black pager sitting in
a black case attached to
a black leather belt

he sports a black watch

talks loudly on a black cell phone
incessantly clicking a black pen...

    black thoughts.

chit

Baby Bumpy

Baby Bumpy
Is getting all thumpy
N' banging around inside of her mummy

She's getting all jumpy
N' wiggling her rumpy
N' stretching out mummy's poor little tummy

But lately she's grumpy
N' down in a slumpy
Cause the food in mummy's tummy's not yummy

It's way too lumpy
Clotted n' clumpy
"It's time for some womb service that isn't so crummy"

So Daddy Dumpy
Best get off his humpy
Instead of sittin' there actin' all chummy

Cause mummy's tummy's not yummy, it's crummy
"Go get some good food you great big ol' dummy!"

Yet under an Angel's unseen tutelage
the outcast child, enchanted by the sun,
will recognize in all he eats and drinks
golden ambrosia and nectar of the gods.

With winds for playmate and with clouds for nurse,
he sings the very stations of his cross –
the Spirit who attends his pilgrimage
weeps to see him happy as a bird.
—Charles Baudelaire
Les Fleurs du Mal

Baudelaire's Angel

Oh God, send Baudelaire's angel
to the blameless side of my little girl
to walk with her in the soundless moments
in between
and whisper love in life and art
in spite of clamoring influences.

Oh God, send Baudelaire's angel
to shepherd her increasing days
that she might someday relish
the taste of ambrosia
and raise a stem of nectar to the heavens
in a silent nod to the other truth.

Flying

Another flying dream.
I've had them all my life.

But this time
my baby girl flew too.

At first, my heart
pounded with fear

at that increased rate
that prunes our years.

But I soon realized
she was fine.

She swirled and turned
gracefully—

Then softly came to rest
in my arms.

But only
for a while.

On waking, I understood
all the useless no's.

Her World

Purple elephants
Sway in blue fields
Of canary grass.

Green whales
Sound in pink oceans
Under a yellow sky.

White birds
Sit in orange trees
With copper trunks
And silver fruit.

The Lucky Sock

I was the lucky sock today
Who from the dryer snuck away

Never again to have to eat
My owner's smelly, sweaty feet

I hid behind the detergent box
With all the other single socks

Hoping I'd be safe back there
Until he bought a brand new pair

A few days later, I froze at the sound
The box was moving, I knew I was found

He saw me, grabbed me 'n started to shout
He acted all crazy 'n waved me about

"I don't believe it!" I heard him say
"I JUST threw your matching sock away!"

Revived

Halloween died for me
many years ago,
a ship in the ocean's belly,
more salt than wood.

Thanksgiving and Christmas
followed soon after,
two aged travelers
who seem to have lost the star.

False expectations?
I don't know.
Cynicism maybe?
No—definitely.

But, a bright-eyed
sixteen-month-old
girl with pom-poms
brings it all back.

I'm a child again.
I believe again.
I revel, romp,
laugh and cry again.

I hope. I love.
I think I understand this time.
I wait and wonder
if it's not too late.

○❖○❖○❖○❖○❖○❖○❖○❖○❖○❖○❖
○   the seeds of life
○   two little aqua eyes
○   like a cherry on top
○   her head pops up
○❖○❖○❖○❖○❖○❖○❖○❖○❖○❖○❖
○   in a mint-swirled blanket
○   a dollop of Cool Whip
○   is Joy herself
○   on the very top
○❖○❖○❖○❖○❖○❖○❖○❖○❖○❖○❖
○   the minty icing on the cake
○   a flowing seafoam green
○   a final layer of bumper pad
○❖○❖○❖○❖○❖○❖○❖○❖○❖○❖○❖
○   of the light 'n fluffy mattress cover
○   the lemon yellow flannel
○   on top of that rests
○❖○❖○❖○❖○❖○❖○❖○❖○❖○❖○❖
○   purple, pink, yellow, and blue
○ flowers 'n butterflies
○ with candy-sprinkled
○ the almond dust ruffle
○❖○❖○❖○❖○❖○❖○❖○❖○❖○❖○❖
○ on moth-colored carpet
○against the flat-white walls
her little ivory bed
○❖○❖○❖○❖○❖○❖○❖○❖○❖○❖○❖

Sweet Cakes

din

Aliya

in the belly of a Boeing whale,
having waited all their lives,
they wait for the mouth to y a w n.

squinting eyes
meet a Mediterranean blaze.
burning nostrils
relish turbine fumes
foreshadowing Judean winds.

canvas bags
and wobbling canes
stream down Jacob's Ladder
to embrace again
Canaan's fiery shores.

tears soak oily pavement
sprouting grace through cracks.
Noah's dormant rainbow returns
with a long forgotten promise.

clasped hands
uplifted eyes
cry—

"Ha Aretz Yisrael!

    I am home…"

All Hayell!

All hail! The Southern Baptist Convention
O blessed brotherhood of rectal retention

A Christian majority   A moral coalition
A liberal purging of all moderation

We tirelessly seek   defemination
And by our behavior   disprove evolution

"They'll know we are Christians by our litigations
By our love   and literal   interpretations"

"By devout duress we'll amass congregations
Consuming the lost in mass conflagrations"

Then up from the ashes will rise exclamations
Uplifted glasses   divine salutations—

"To original texts!   and infallibation!
All hayell! The Southern Baptist Convention!"

Guns & Rabbis

M-16's

hanging

bumping

chamber full

ready

waiting

black hats

bobbing

up and down

back and forth

pages flapping

in a breeze

of chant and

repetition

Jericho

it
  is
a long
and bumpy
road   down
thru terra cotta
mountains past
goat skin tents with
TV antennas n' a pepto-
pink Mercedes   its wheels
              to the sky

hundreds of feet   below sea level
air so thick it does the breathing for me
burning   ripping thru open windows
sanding down my face   tugging at my hair

my shirt is soaked   stuck to the seat-back
              my right arm sunburned

the town is shut down   orders of the PLO   a
floundering demonstration   eons of frustration
Yassir Are ya' fat and getting old   ah hell, I'll have
                    piece o' that prize too

our favorite little restaurant   meaningfully blown to
bits by anger beaming down from a merciless Judean sun

John the Southern Baptist

I slip into the hallway

   behind the sanctuary,

      when suddenly   a voice

                                        calling

scripture,   out

from little white speakers   in the

ceiling—mounted,

      bounces off

         brick walls painted   desert—

      white—

"Repent!"

echoes   -es   -es

coming to rest

in the mottled blue carpet.   "Repent!"

May Day
Saturday – May 1, 1999

black Nike Airs set a quick pace
untanned calves flash in sunlight
a saffron robe with brown tasseled belt
    flaps down the side of I-35
wire-frame glasses struggle to support
    a concerned cro-magnon brow
brown bushy hair tries
    to cover the shiny cue ball

a stoic shoulder
    harnessed with a nine foot cross—
        black rubber wheel attached to the bottom—
        Wal-Mart special

a sign on the back of the cross roars at traffic
    coming up behind:

    GOD WANTS
      PRAYER
      BACK IN
      SCHOOL

and I'm thinkin'—

                      Jesus didn't get a wheel

Southern-Fried-Sundays

Mine was a
Sunday-after-church-fried-chicken-childhood.
Cornbread-n'-squash-casserole-afternoons gave way
to mandarin-orange-Jello-salad-sunsets.
Sweet-potato-evenings by roasted-marshmallow-fires
always left time for devil'd-egg-stories
n' home-made-ice-cream-tunes.
Guitars were the nuts n' chocolate sauce
of unenforced bed times.

It was a mythical age when fam'lies stuck together
like day-old-steamed-white-rice.
And laughter was as simple as a tipped-over-lawn-chair
      and ashes on the end of a burnt hot dog.

Baptists'll tell ya' "*church* is ever'thing."
But they all know without saying—
God is in the food
and licked fingers
of a Sunday after noon.

Sunday Morning

I snuck out of the service
after playing guitar—
though, I did wait 'til the children sang
since Jesus seems to think
they touch the face of God

nothing against the preacher
I mean
the church smelled like a good enough place

but a poet beckoned
and I had to read again
Linda McCarriston's
"A Castle in Lynn"
and cry with her for a while
     and   for my ex-wife
          and for the thousands of memories
            that separate them from their fathers

yes
it was the poet
    not the preacher
who rang the bells
in my hopeful little village this morning

The Wailing Wall

I hear the wall wailing
from the weight of our prayers
that eternally prick its millennial cracks

I hear the wall wailing
from the ageless torment
of war and destruction and unending tears

It cries to the east,
"blind-hinged hatred has abandoned your souls"

It cries to the west,
"the sleep of complacency has hooded your eyes"

I hear the wall wailing
it cries to me now,
"embrace the blood of my murdered children"

I hear
            the wall
                        wailing

moot

A Few Good Lines

a h h hell…
          …gotta write a poem
…need somethin' h e r e…
… need an opening line…
    ("ahh hell's" not bad though)
…damn…
what 'm I thinkin'?…
I'm thinkin'…
I got other things to be doin'…
I'm thinkin'…
a h h hell
not every one of 'em's gonna
rip the roof off the arena you idiot…
…move on…

        …500 poems
                n' a few good lines.

Anything Goes

But! —
don't moralize
don't tell — show
don't explain
describe more
      "Prufrock me in the bosom of Abraham"
cut it
add it
rewrite it
make it more like…
I can't see…
where's the conflict?
read more of … then…
drama
foreplay
time line
cliché
closure
      see   smell   hear   taste   feel
develop
establish
let the reader…
    Detail! Detail! Detail!
        but other than that…

Award

I received an award today
in the Union Ballroom.
The Chamber of Commerce
decided to distinguish me
as an artist.

The speaker was a diplomat,
and most diplomatic,
in a more pleasant way than usual.
I actually found him interesting.
That disturbs me still.

Did the coats and ties get to me?
Did I take a bite
of the Bourgeois Burger
and like it?

Well, I don't know.
But I accepted the award.

I'm not that much of a
frickin' artistic idiot.

Coffee

I just drank coffee
I never drink coffee

it's a reception
for academiacs

I suppose the coffee
makes me feel more academic
or at least ephemerally endemic

anyway

they're all drinking it
and they seem to know a lot of stuff

Compound Spiral

...dry run	..........dry
down town	run down
hall way	town hall
faring well	way faring
water snake	well water
oil lamp	snake oil
shade tree	lamp shade
house guest	tree house
bed room	guest bed
service man	room service
power play	man power
back bone	play back
dry..........	bone dry...

Emotion in Music
— a seminar

I understood her prepositions
the definitions of many words
but how they all connected
to make useful sentences
is anyone's guess

personality and feeling
offered on the altar
of form and content

she knew terribly much
    about the subject matter
but her fingers
had obviously
never plucked the strings
she had never
placed a cheek
on the ebony gloss while playing

she kept talking
blinking and smiling
spouting
the biggest bag of academic bovine feces—

is there *emotion* in the *music* it*self?*

    What   the   hell   kind   of   question   is   that?

A Fitting End

my notepad slipped
    into the bowl of gravy
a burial at sea

a fitting end
    to carelessly penned
amateur poetry

Gematrias

FIRE
Tell us of
　An old and
　　Tall, tall tale

　　　　　　　BEING
　　　　　　A pen and
　　　　　　 Page to
　　　　　　　Speak of
　　　　　　　Wages I
　　　　　　　 Must pay as a
　　　　　　　　nu poet

DOG STEW
A yellow
　Taco Mayo
　　As the old
　　 Cat flies

　　　　　　　UNDERWHELMED
　　　　　　Rush Limbaugh's a
　　　　　　 Self-labeled guru

Hobson's Choice

I sit
`A W H I T E A M E R I C A N M A L E`
in my little Barnes & Noble Bookstore
`B I B L E B E L T M I D D L E C L A S S`
with my little pen and pad
`C A R H O U S E D O G K I D W I F E`
and try to birth a golden language.

I fear
`W O R K 8 H O U R D A Y S W E E K E N D S O F F`
however   —   I have
`P A R E N T S M A R R I E D A N D H A P P Y`
no axe-wielding trial
    worthy of CNN
no dripping childhood wound
    from which to muster miserable images
no inherited holocaust
    raging me to remembrance

I have
`F O O D C L O T H E S T V L A T T E`
    lost no child
    fought no war
    committed no crime

no license
to write

It's versus Its

It's not hard is it
To know when it's time
To use an apostrophe in the word "it's"
And when it's not, to use it in the word "its?"
It's proper in showing its contraction of—"it is."
However, it's not its place in the word "its" when it's
used in its possessive pronoun form — "its."
True, it's used in most other possessive forms.
But it's not in this possessive instance of "its."
"It's his dog." "It's licking its paw." So again,
it *is* "it's" when it's contracting "it is" into "it's."
but it's not "it's" when its use is to show
its possessive nature in its 3rd person
form of "its."   Because,
"its" is its own thing, is it not?
Yes, it's its own thing.
So this is it, is it?
Yes, it's.

Meaning...
(a note to Jon)

don'tpu-
shit
mywi-
de-ey-
ed,gulli-
blefri-
end

whatap-
pearsmy-
sterio-
usn'pro-
found
maysim-
plybeme-
aning-
less

My Question to Freud

So, what is it that forces that index finger
    on my right hand
to reach over and incessantly pick the cuticle
    of my left hand's middle finger
        during class?

Was it the time my parents left me
    at the neighbors when I was four?
Was it the first time I saw my mother cry?
Was it the time…

Or is it that floating baboon gene
carefully honed by evolution
in response to centuries of boredom?

Openings

Did you hear the one about…
So there were these two…
What happens when you cross…
One day, four…
Have you ever noticed…
A guy's sittin' in a bar…
Your mother's so…
A blond goes in a…
Did you ever wonder…

Back when rocks were soft…

Orpheus Sing!

Orpheus sing!
     Sing on, my brother—
     drawing tears
     from Hell's betrothed.

Orpheus sing!
     Sing on, my brother—
     though you look back
     and lose her forever.

Sing!
     Sing on, my brother.

This poem could be:
a)   a 33-piece morphological puzzle
b)   a 33-minute lucubration
c)   a look at movies in the 90s

Point Blank Necrosis
and Fugacious Concupiscence

---

ensanguined corpus
disembogued encephalon
faux soniferous FX
mendaciously salient frames

stripling meets gamine
                              no
stripling does gamine
then laureately absconds
for he could not abide
and asseverate his intrepidity

Key to "Point Blank Necrosis"

Point Blank Murder
and Temporary Sex

bloody bodies
blown out brains
phony sound FX
falsely jumping frames

boy meets girl

                                      no

boy does girl
then righteously leaves
for he could not stay
and still be hero

Rhetoric

        after all of the words
        the nouns and the verbs
        I froze in a moment of dread

for   what seemed to be something
        turned out to be nothing
        no thing had actually been said

so   I hope in some way
        somehow, someday
        before the rolls are read

        to think of a new thing
        and *some*day say *some*thing
        for nothing's already been said

Something

there I was
applauding

                    something

I didn't understand
but
it must have meant

                    something

because
there were people
with glasses
gray hair
and sleek pens
writing

                    something

they're laughing
it must be a

                    fun thing

so I lean forward
looking
as if I'm listening
clasp my hands
beneath my chin
thinking

                    something

The Beast

white male
        small ass
                middle class
                          apology denied
Christian
        republicrat
                castrate
                        kick his ass
guilty
        out of line

but wait…
great grandmother Cherokee
        black blood-brother rescued me
                embrace my femininity
no!
        liar!
                Caucasian he

please…
listen closer to the song
artist—lover
                dream in color

The Villainous Nelle

I held in contempt, yet admired as well
With utmost respect, I secretly hated
The one who created the villainous nelle

The recurring lines, the tenth syllabelle
Impossible rhymes and meters upended
I held in contempt, yet admired as well

Its difficult structure, Gematraic helle
In doing my best, I wriggled and wrested
With the one who created the villainous nelle

Plenty of paper, ink's bottomless welle
A poet with plenty of time to be wasted
I held in contempt, yet admired as well

The lack of TV was easy to telle
In the poetic home of the one whom I hated
The one who created the villainous nelle

They have now padded my artistic celle
From when I combated, cried then decided
I held in contempt, yet admired as welle
The one who created the villainous nelle

rumi

Ah, Thanksgiving

That wonderful time of year
when we cut up all the turkeys
in the family
into scrutinized pieces
when brief moments find us paired off
in bedrooms and bathrooms

Ben Yehuda Street

thick gray fur
appears on the porch
of the back alley café

    her
        tail
            moves
          slowly
      back
     and
       forth

warm chair
by the table
recently vacated
of ice cream groupies

onto the table
    chocolate?   no.
    strawberry?   no.
ahhh...... vanilla.

    her
        tail
            moves
          slowly
      back
     and
       forth

Breath of Life

you extend your hand
to one stepping on your toes
excess   ively w(h)ining of lack

you feed and shelter
one who throws it up in your face
burns it to the ground

I cheat you
say I love you
then deny you
more than twice

yet, you cradle me
staving random death
an undeserving pardon
as I continue drawing you in

The Cool Winds Came

the cool winds came
for the third time this spring
the heat crept backwards
and sat on its haunches

I think I felt Atlas's shoulders relax
and the soul
of the dwellers
sigh

Cool, Cloudy

there's something about a cool, cloudy day
that flies in the face of an Oklahoma August
and pulls me by the T-shirt
out the front door

the breeze prods me down old footpaths
to a picture frame of youth—
the Westwood Park golf course and public pool

i step across the old drainage ditch
i used to have to jump
and i'm hijacked by nostalgic visions
of knobby bicycle tires on blacktop pavement,
    the bright juicy red of skinned knees and elbows,
    dandelion plumes fluffing through the air,
    and the bitter sweet of bumble-bees
        among the honeysuckle

i traipse across a dew drenched fairway
chuckling about golf lessons i took when i was 12—
one of those crazy, lazy dreams
of avoiding a real job
as i'm doing to this day

my nostrils flair while passing by
the chlorine smell of the swimming pool
it mixes with the muggy, blue-gray air
and tones the newly stretched canvas
    while
my mind fills in the empty towels

with hot — oily — sun-quenched
    — hormone-infested bodies

aahhh. the profound apocalyptic confusion
of growing up in the buckle of the bible belt

i move on to the more innocent sidewalk
that carried my hormones and daydreams home
remembering the blazing concrete
that burned my bare feet
and made me jump into the patchy grass
risking a sticker or two

i remember the feel of the cool, cloudy creek
that soothing chill on a warm day
rich melting chocolate
oozing up between toes

perch shining in the breezy light
wriggling, writhing, then relaxing
for a moment
    like a wet silver dollar pancake
while i work out the hook

water color
changing with every stage of the sun
a Winslow Homer in eternal renewal
    and ever shifting shades

the walk home reminds me of smuggled adventures
forged in the cool, cloudy nights.

running from the growl of the greens-keeper's truck
while he cursed me on a late night patrol
or becoming, myself   the unimagined terror
of others who didn't belong

my chest would swell   in a silent howl
towards the half of the moon that was showing
the dreams in my eyes could blow out its flame
if i let them loose through the thinning air

Depression

Tired a lot—

                              sleepy.

Gotta do somethin'…

gotta—

                cut back on sugar I suppose.

Damn.

                    Why can't broccoli taste good?

Evening

another sun-sink evening
glimmers on a soft-shouldered line
slipping off boots
before an unseasonal fire

The Plains

the wind slaps
a flap of green canvas
against a rotting door frame

Green Lady

It was that "green lady" on Star Trek
who ravaged my budding hormones.
Don't remember a plot.
Just that twitching, salty dance.　　But

it wasn't gyration or bulging shapes
or eyes like eggs in salad…
…maybe the blazing white of teeth
…or the flash of pink in the tongue.

But absolutely—

it was that smooth green skin
like a peeled avocado
I knew would slip between fingers
and smell of mint, sage, or seawater.

I felt my confused body stir.
I burned to know the forbidden:
"Does the green reach up inside,
beneath those barely clothes?"

Night Game

Maybe it's those lights
holding on to Joshua's sun
and fans dressed against the cold
like dutiful soldiers
wiggling toes and fingers
to keep a flow of blood
while hunkered in the hole.

Or maybe it's that stadium hotdog
you have to take your gloves off to eat,
its warmth bypassing thoughts
of animal by-products.
You gotta lick the ketchup
and mustard off fingers,
cause there ain't no way
you're gonna stick 'em under
that ice cold tap
in the men's urinal barn,
never to feel them again.

Maybe it's the way
you hold that cup of hot chocolate
between both hands,
a sacred drink offering
raised to angry sport gods
in hopes your team won't
get its ass kicked this time.
Of course,
the cup takes a pit stop
at chapped but grateful lips
on the way up.

Or maybe
it's about believing—
that never-ending hope
that somehow,
some way,
even though you're 3 and 8,
fate, taking a night off,
will crinkle a corner of its mouth,
and your team will win.

Perception

is it merely a pat of soft butter,
or the crowning of life's next moment?

is it a sliced cinnamon-raisin bagel,
or the glory of daily ceremony?

is it a musty, rough-hewn table
   a squeaking chair
      a mottled steel knife
         and a filmy wood-frame window,
or   space   engorged with meaning
   fraught with motionless desire?

are they merely evening rays,
or divine hands stretching?

Sunset Symphony

....

....

......

the clouds are settling

into their places

the breeze is tuning

up   to middle sea

...

....

and the sun is dimming the lights

......

...

the curtain raises

and gilded rays

shoot across the sky

a path of golden light

leaps across the water

as sand and surf

roar with applause

......

...

Turkey Day

The season is upon us now,
With its usual foul weather.
Yet we make it home somehow,
Come crashing back together.

The reason is never talked about,
Because no one understands
Our desire for tension, stress and doubt,
Betrayed by white-knuckled hands.

Just once I'd love to let 'em have it,
Pull my finger from the dyke
And bust wide open this annual habit,
Let streams of consciousness strike.

Exploding turkey, splattered pie,
My siblings strewn all about.
N' those they married with blackened eye
Would proceed to scream and shout.

This unexpected honesty
Would blow our world apart.
But oh, that healing alchemy
Of laying bare the heart.

Wordless

I'm on one of those walks
    one of those too-much-sodium-
        cholesterol-stress-you're-dying walks

my body warms
    to the falling orange of the horizon
    and the pace of my feet
my Reeboks scratch the sidewalk
    as a bass breaks the surface
    of the wind rippled pond

I stop dead in my tracks
    when
jutting from the end of a leafless branch
the silhouette of The Great Blue Heron
    head turning
        beak pointing
straight at my cranium

centuries away
I'm blown through a chrono-canon

he beams his wordless message
directly into my soul

something along the lines of

    s l o w   d o w n